Helicopter Man

Igor Sikorsky and His Amazing Invention

Edwin Brit Wyckoff

Enslow Elementary

an imprint of

Enslow Publishers, Inc.

40 Industrial Road
Box 398
Berkeley Heights, NJ 07922
USA

http://www.enslow.com

Content Adviser
Ned Barnett
Aviation historian and author

Series Literacy Consultant
Allan A. De Fina, PhD
Dean, College of Education and Professor of Literacy Education
New Jersey City University
Past President of the New Jersey Reading Association

Enslow Elementary, an imprint of Enslow Publishers, Inc.

Enslow Elementary® is a registered trademark of Enslow Publishers, Inc.

Library of Congress Cataloging-in-Publication Data

Wyckoff, Edwin Brit.
  Helicopter man : Igor Sikorsky and his amazing invention / Edwin Brit Wyckoff.
     p. cm. — (Genius at work! Great inventor biographies)
  Includes bibliographical references and index.
  Summary: "Read about Igor Sikorsky's life, and how he built the first successful helicopter"—Provided by publisher.
  ISBN-13: 978-0-7660-3445-7
  ISBN-10: 0-7660-3445-3
  1. Sikorsky, Igor Ivan, 1889–1972—Juvenile literature. 2. Aeronautical engineers—United States—Biography
—Juvenile literature. 3. Aeronautical engineers—Russia (Federation)—Biography—Juvenile literature.
4. Helicopters—History—Juvenile literature. 5. Aeronautics—History—Juvenile literature. I. Title.
  TL540.S54W93 2010
  629.130092—dc22
  [B]
                                    2009015881

Printed in the United States of America

072010 Lake Book Manufacturing, Inc., Melrose Park, IL

10 9 8 7 6 5 4 3 2 1

To Our Readers
We have done our best to make sure all Internet addresses in this book were active and appropriate when we went to press. However, the author and the publisher have no control over and assume no liability for the material available on those Internet sites or on other Web sites they may link to. Any comments or suggestions can be sent by e-mail to comments@enslow.com or to the address on the back cover.

♻ Enslow Publishers, Inc., is committed to printing our books on recycled paper. The paper in every book contains 10% to 30% post-consumer waste (PCW). The cover board on the outside of each book contains 100% PCW. Our goal is to do our part to help young people and the environment too!

Every effort has been made to locate all copyright holders of material used in this book. If any errors or omissions have occurred, corrections will be made in future editions of this book.

Contents

Igor Sikorsky

Chapter 1

Midnight Madness

Igor Sikorsky saw himself walking along a hallway lined with dark, shining wood. There were soft blue lights overhead. The thick carpet beneath his feet rumbled and shook. Sikorsky was walking in the sky in a great big flying machine that began to roll over and dive down, down, down. His eyes flew wide open. But the dream stayed with him until it became part of his real life.

Igor Sikorsky (sih-KORE-skee) was born on May 25, 1889, in Kiev, Russia. Today Kiev is the capital of a country called Ukraine. Igor's father, Ivan, was a doctor and professor. His mother, Zinaida, stayed home to care for Igor, his older sisters, Lydia, Olga, and Elena, and his younger

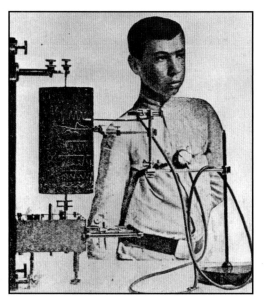

Igor Sikorsky at twelve, with equipment used to measure blood pressure. From a young age, Sikorsky was interested in science.

brother, Sergei. The family lived in a big house with a wonderful garden.

Young Igor had his own workshop in a small cottage in the garden. He built toys driven by electric motors. His mother showed him drawings made hundreds of years earlier by the great artist and inventor Leonardo da Vinci. One sketch showed a circular flying machine that had no wings. It was a fascinating idea.

When Igor was only fourteen, he entered the Russian Naval Academy. At seventeen, he switched to studying engineering at a technical school in Kiev. Then he saw a picture of the

6

Wright brothers with their airplane. Later he said: "Within twenty-four hours, I decided to change my life's work. I would study aviation." After a trip to Paris to talk with French pilots about building airplanes, the eighteen-year-old moved home to Kiev. Every day he disappeared into his workshop in the garden for hours and

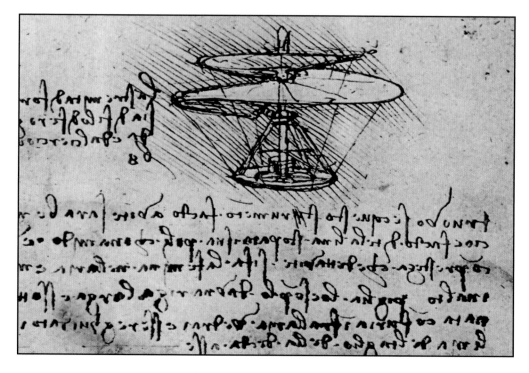

Leonardo da Vinci's sketch for a helicopter. (Leonardo's writing is backward, a method he often used.)

A painting showing the historic flight of the Wright Brothers

hours. Finally he roared out on the steam-powered motorcycle he had built.

Next, Igor focused on building a wingless flying machine like Leonardo's. His sister Olga lent him money for an engine he had seen in France. Both of them believed he could invent a helicopter that could fly. Not everyone did.

Helicopters do many jobs today.
Until Igor Sikorsky came along,
they were only a dream.

Even Wilbur Wright, one of the great American inventors of the airplane, said that helicopters would never work. The unstoppable Igor designed a helicopter called the H-1. It shook, rattled, and scampered across his garden. It never lifted off the ground. He invented another, the H-2, that struggled up a few inches, but could not lift him at all. Frustrated, Igor pushed those thoughts about inventing helicopters way back in his head. That game seemed to be over and gone forever.

Chapter 2

The Murderous Mosquito

In 1910 Sikorsky was twenty-one years old and ready to design, build, and fly his own airplane. The plane he designed had an engine pushing from behind. It went racing across a field. But it would not lift his weight into the air. Failure did not stop Sikorsky. It seemed to make him work harder. He always had another idea and the courage to try it. A plumber and a bicycle repairman offered to help him pull apart the plane and move the motor up front. Sikorsky sailed a thousand feet into the air, wild with happiness. In 1912, one of his planes won first prize at an air show in Moscow, Russia. He

Sikorsky with his second helicopter, the H-2. Like the H-1, it was not successful.

seemed as natural as a bird riding waves of air or zooming down to wave at his friends.

In the middle of one high-speed zoom, the engine stalled. There was nothing but deadly silence. His plane spiraled toward the earth and crash-landed, but Sikorsky walked away unhurt. His friends helped pull apart the engine. They

The photo on Sikorsky's Russian pilot's license, issued in 1911

found one dead mosquito blocking a tiny gas line. If one tiny mosquito could stop one big engine, it made sense to have more engines. Sikorsky learned that there was safety in numbers.

A railroad car factory hired Sikorsky to build a single-engine plane that was good enough to win an air race. The head of the company invited Sikorsky to dinner. Sikorsky told him of his belief in the safety of planes with more than one engine—multiengine planes. He pushed harder by suggesting that if they won the race, they should use the prize money to build a multiengine plane. His boss stopped Igor. He said they should not wait. They should start building it immediately.

Sikorsky in his office at the railroad car factory, where he was hired to build a fast single-engine plane

With almost no time to sleep or eat, Sikorsky camped out in an old shipping crate at the factory. His small crew built the *Grand*, which had three engines and a wingspan of 92 feet (28 meters). Passengers could actually stand in the sky on an open deck with 60-mile-per-hour (97-kilometer-per-hour) winds whipping around them. It was a stunning success. Sikorsky was ordered to build a larger plane immediately.

The new giant *Ilia Mourometz* was named after an ancient Russian hero. Its wings stretched out 102 feet (31 meters). Its luxurious cabin had

The *Ilia Mourometz*, the world's first four-engine plane, was named for a hero from Russian history.

four very comfortable seats and a washroom. A hallway with dark, shining wooden walls had thick carpeting underfoot. Blue lights hung overhead. The midnight madness Sikorsky had dreamed up years ago flew beautifully in broad daylight. He was still in his twenties, and his career was flying high.

Chapter 3

Flying Boats

In 1914, World War I exploded across Europe. Sikorsky's luxury airliners were turned into Russian bombers. Losing battle after battle, the Russians burned their own planes on the ground to stop the enemy from capturing them. During that terrible time, years of Sikorsky's hard work became heaps of ashes.

In 1917 the Russian Revolution rolled across the land. The government collapsed. Many families lost their fortunes. Igor Sikorsky

This photograph of Sikorsky was taken when he was twenty-six years old.

fled to France and was hired to design a bomber. But when World War I ended in 1918, Sikorsky's job ended too. There was no future for him in Europe. He sailed for New York City in 1919 with less than six hundred dollars in his pocket.

Sikorsky had no job and knew almost no English. He lived on beans and bread while teaching math and science to newly arrived Russians. And he talked endlessly about inventing new airplanes. His students offered to work on them without pay. They set out to find people with money to invest in building airplanes. And they succeeded. On March 5, 1923, Sikorsky opened the Sikorsky Aero Engineering Corporation on a farm on Long Island, New York. The chicken house was turned into an office and workshop. A plane was assembled in what had been an old barn.

Everybody worked ten to twelve hours a day. Some searched for parts in junkyards.

Finally, the workers and investors watched their plane rise into the sky—then watched it crash-land minutes later. They had nothing left—no plane, no money, and no jobs. Sikorsky later said: "The greatest danger in aviation was starvation."

Workers at the first Sikorsky plant on Long Island, New York. They worked long hours, sometimes getting materials from junkyards.

He called a meeting of investors, locked the doors, and demanded that they come up with twenty-five hundred dollars. He won them over with a powerful speech. Then he rebuilt the plane so it was strong enough to carry two huge pianos from New York to Washington, D.C. One piano was for the wife of the president of the United States. Spirits soared. But the need for planes was sagging. The end of Sikorsky's American adventure seemed to be coming fast.

Sikorsky did not give up. He always had a better, bigger invention. This time it was a huge, multiengine flying boat that could take off from water and land on water. It did not need expensive airports with huge runways. His flying boats could cross oceans, landing in lakes, rivers, and harbors almost anywhere. In 1928 he began building them for the U.S. Navy and for Pan American World Airways. There was a hallway

Sikorsky's seaplane—or "flying boat"—could take off and land in water.

inside with dark, shining, wooden walls and thick carpeting underfoot. Blue lights hung overhead. It was his dream coming true again.

Business soared. Sikorsky's company became part of United Aircraft, which later became United Technologies. Then, in 1929, thousands of businesses shut down in the Great Depression. Fear gripped the country. But Igor Sikorsky always fought fear with a new idea.

Chapter 4

Flying Without Wings

Sikorsky's business was just about smashed to pieces. He had married Elizabeth Semion, another Russian immigrant, in 1924. They had five children—four sons and one daughter—to support. This amazing man had an amazing idea stuffed way back in his memory: Helicopters did not need runways. They could rise straight up into the air, moving up and down, turning in any direction. It was his impossible dream. So he tackled the tough job of finding money to build his helicopter. Fortunately, people had a hard time saying "no" to Sikorsky.

United Aircraft finally gave him thirty thousand dollars to turn a collection of metal

Sikorsky flies the VS-300.

pipes into a helicopter. He tested it and tore it apart so often his team called the machine "Igor's Nightmare." But on September 14, 1939, he climbed aboard the VS-300. It shook, rattled, and lifted off beautifully. Sikorsky steered the helicopter by tipping the angle of its rotor blades.

How a Helicopter Flies

The **main rotor** blades cut through the air, letting the machine climb into the sky or hover in one spot. As the blades spin, the body of the helicopter tries to spin in the other direction.

The **tail rotor** keeps the body from spinning out of control. It can guide the ship left and right.

The pilot tilts the angle of the blades to steer the flying machine up, down, or in any direction.

Tail rotor

Main rotor

On May 13, 1940, Sikorsky popped his soft gray hat, called a fedora, onto his head. It was his lucky charm. Newspaper reporters came to see his "nightmare" climb into the sky. For one hour and thirty-two minutes the helicopter hung in the air. It turned circles, went backward and sideways, but it never went forward. Luck flew with him that day. Not one of the reporters asked him to fly forward. He invented forward flight later on.

22

Sikorsky in his VS-300, the first working helicopter, in May 1940

Chapter 5

Dare to Dream

World War II had been tearing Europe apart since 1939. In July 1941, the U.S. Army ordered one test helicopter. On December 7, 1941, the United States was plunged into the war when Pearl Harbor in Hawaii was bombed by Japanese forces. A few weeks later, Sikorsky stuck his lucky gray fedora on his head and flew his two-seater helicopter in a perfect demonstration for the generals. At one point, he hovered over a Connecticut roadway, leaning down to ask drivers for directions back to the factory. It was scary. It was fun. And it made history.

Igor Sikorsky was the first to use a single rotor to lift and steer his machine. His helicopter

The first U.S. Army helicopter flies past the U.S. Capitol building in 1942.

FACT

Helicopters are workhorses in the sky:

- Rescuing people

- Herding animals

- Exploring and mapping the earth

- Firefighting

- Lifting huge loads

- Carrying troops and equipment

- Directing traffic

- Chasing criminals

- Carrying food and machinery to oil rigs in the ocean

- Carrying skiers to the slopes

- Finding submarines and chasing them

- Shuttling the U.S. president from the White House lawn to Air Force One

was the first to go into mass production. His company has been building the fantastic flying machines longer than any other. One of them picked up the first U.S. astronaut, Alan Shepard, when his space capsule landed in the ocean.

Inventing the helicopter was Igor Sikorsky's greatest accomplishment. This Russian, who became an American citizen, loved the idea of freedom: freedom to invent, freedom to take risks, even freedom to fail and fight back to the top again.

He had dared to build multiengine planes, flying boats, and machines that could fly without wings. And in 1968 the president of the United States, Lyndon B. Johnson, gave him the golden National Medal of Science.

This quiet genius died at age eighty-three on October 26, 1972, at his home in Connecticut.

Sikorsky in his famous lucky fedora

Pilots from around the world had often asked Sikorsky if they could wear his good-luck fedora for just a few seconds. Sikorsky would smile.

He never, ever, said no.

Timeline

1889   Born May 25 in Kiev, a city in Ukraine, then part of the Russian Empire.

1909–1910 Builds two helicopters in home workshop; neither one flies successfully.

1910   Builds biplane.

1912   Takes job with Russian railroad company to build airplane for a race; wins first prize in Moscow.

1913   Builds large multiengine plane called the *Grand*.

1914   Builds larger airliner called the *Ilia Mourometz*; Russians turn it into a bomber during World War I.

1917   Russian Revolution forces Sikorsky to move to France and design bombers there; job ends when World War I ends.

1919   Moves to New York City; teaches math and science.

1923   Opens Sikorsky Aero Engineering Corporation on old farm in Long Island.

1924   Marries Elizabeth Semion; they have four children.

1928   Builds large "Flying Boats" for U.S. Navy and an airline.

1939   Designs first successful helicopter, the VS-300.

1972   Dies October 26 at his home in Easton, Connecticut.

Words to Know

aviation—The science or practice of flying aircraft.

bomber—A plane that carries bombs to drop on the enemy.

engineering—A career in which a person uses scientific knowledge to design, build, and operate machinery and manufacturing systems.

fedora—A man's soft felt hat with a brim that can be turned up or down.

investor—Someone who puts money into a business or project and expects to earn money if it succeeds or lose money if it fails.

mass production—A very quick system for building large numbers of things such as cars, phones, or television sets.

multiengine plane—A plane with more than one engine.

rotors—A circular group of blades that lifts and guides helicopters. Some use one rotor that lies flat. Others use two rotors that stand up. These are called tilt-rotors.

wingspan—The length of an airplane wing from tip to tip.

Books

Clements, Gillian. *The Picture History of Great Inventors*. London: Frances Lincoln Children's Books, 2005.

Goodman, Susan E. *Choppers!* New York: Random House Books for Young Readers, 2004.

Nahum, Andrew. *Flying Machine*. New York: Dorling Kindersley Ltd., 2004.

Otfinoski, Steven. *Igor Sikorsky: Father of the Helicopter*. Vero Beach, Fla.: Rourke Enterprises, 1993.

Internet Addresses

Helicopter History Site
http://www.helis.com

Igor I. Sikorsky Historical Archives
http://www.sikorskyarchives.com

U.S. Centennial of Flight Commission: Rotary Flight
http://www.centennialofflight.gov/essay_cat/4.htm

Index